Overallness.
Field drawing, territory series; No. 0102: plan.

SERIAL BOOKS
Architecture & Urbanism 2

Field Event/Field Space

Kevin Rhowbotham

Globular Field Distribution.
Field drawing, territory Series; No. 0122: plan.

Field Event

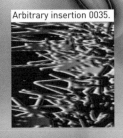

Arbitrary insertion 0035.

concerning field, territory, traject

swarming in event space — five

for the extension of architectural

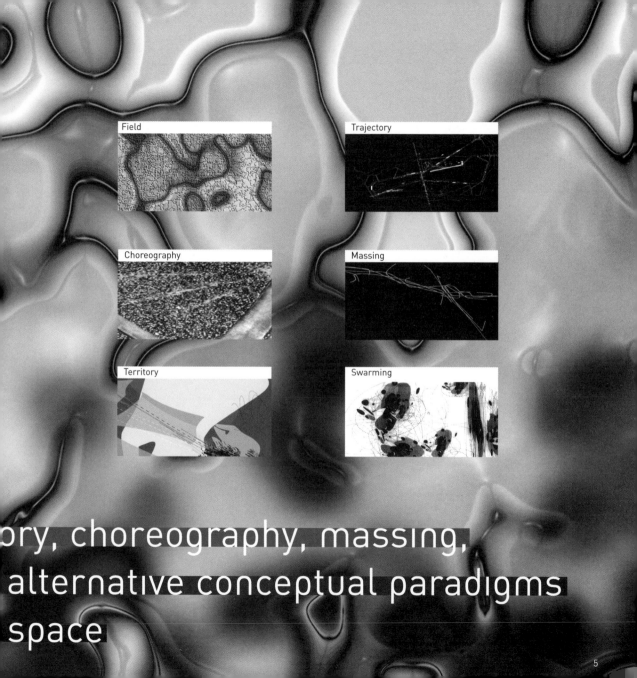

Field

Trajectory

Choreography

Massing

Territory

Swarming

ory, choreography, massing,
alternative conceptual paradigms
space

Field drawing, territory series; No. 0773: plan.

impact upon architecture itself. It would be altogether unsurprising to assert therefore, that the main body of the architectural profession — the inconsistent and heterogeneous contributions of its erstwhile avant-gardist margins notwithstanding — has refused, thus far, any fundamental and critical re-alignment with emergent cultural conditions, preferring the ostensible permanence of abstract form over the uncertainties and complexities of cultural content.

Indeed, the profession seems to have surrendered all pretensions to any possible critique of cultural values, arguing meekly that it must remain an independent institution beyond dirty politics. Disingenuousness aside, this position offers no means by which a productive programmatics might be materially refashioned. No means by which the conditions of use, of inhabitation, that is to say

In the contemporary architectural debate, an impasse is reached when questions of value arise. Most particularly when value is considered in relation to emancipatory content, critical self-appraisal or the ultimate social purpose of architectural work. The possibility of establishing a debate which is focused on the values of architecture, on its ethical end point or teleology is often resisted avoided or blocked, but always considered unnecessary, since mother architecture, we are told, is primarily a **profession**, a non-aligned, non-political body, having its own, self-referential ethical codes and standards.

Whether this be true for all architects, it is certainly true enough to ensure that the debates which have raged in other disciplines, concerning the fragmentation of singular cultural perspectives and their subsequent imposition upon current practice, have made little

of programme, might be repositioned at the centre, rather than at the periphery of a productive and engaged architectural practice. The a-social superfluities of the 80s and early 90s, which fostered the re-establishment of laissez-faire commodity exchange, brokered a market in architectural styling the like of which has not been seen since the indiscriminate plagiarisms and social theatricality of Victorian pomp. It left architecture as a productive, culturally incisive practice, sadly lacking in initiative; altogether disconnected from the consequent realities and material transformations of the contemporary city.

If the profession is to venture a reconstruction of its tenuous connection with the material realities of the city, with the intellectual ground of its own means of production, then it must, and urgently, forge an altogether new and materially pertinent programmatics.

Architectural journalism and historical commentary, the self proclaimed critical arm of the profession, have proved themselves poorly prepared to lead such a structural revision. They remain coarse, blunt, even procrustean instruments, proscribing the structures of architectural production by lumbering acts of reduction and **dumbing down**. New directions in architecture which have undertaken such a critique, although rare, have found themselves abruptly recuperated. This cynical trade of commentary, which would "... die laughing to think itself serious..." (Kraus), far from presenting sober exposition seeks only to convert unorthodox ideas and initiatives into legitimate, consumable terms in order to proliferate its own abject existence. Criticism, debate, not to say politically motivated campaigning itself, although desperately needed to revitalise, even to re-invent a material architectural programmatics pertinent to the problems of the contemporary city, are conspicuously absent from the formulaic copy of popular architectural journals.

Soft commentary has replaced hard journalism, abetting a culture of quietness, deference and self-censorship. An entirely fraudulent social decorum, the product of a mealy-mouthed a-political and thoroughly glacial professionalism, has constructed a context in which it is now **impolite** to criticise the work of others no matter how venal or downright irresponsible it might be.

Debate concerning the long term aims and goals of the profession, constructive of teleologies which might just usher in new initiatives for dealing with emerging urban conditions, have long since evaporated into that ubiquitous ether of short-termism, expedient pragmatics and commodity potlatch, currently masquerading as the culture of architecture.

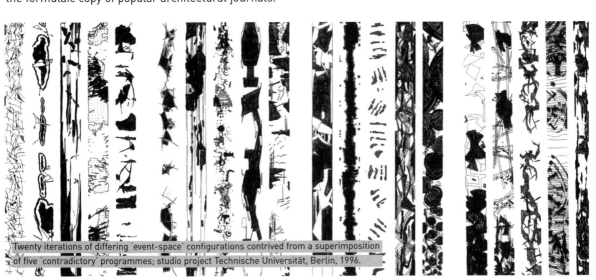

Twenty iterations of differing 'event-space' configurations contrived from a superimposition of five 'contradictory' programmes; studio project Technische Universität, Berlin, 1996.

SPATIAL POLITICS NOT THE POLITICS OF SPACE

If we are to assume that architecture does not define itself as a covert solipsism. That it does not fall into an easy idealism and assume that its definitive qualities are intrinsic to the objects of its production and not consequent upon the contexts of its production. If we are to assume that it relies, not merely on the fact of architecture as physical mass, but also upon an audience to experience it; that it constitutes more than an internally determined problematic; that it remains grounded in the complexities of everyday life, its politics, economics and material conditions, then it must follow that the **meaning** of architecture, the sense that it makes for us, is constituted from at least two phenomena. Not only the object; **the physical displacement of matter in space**; but also the event; **the muti-valent, multi-layered social perception of objects in use**.

It was the Situationist International which initiated a comprehensive revaluation of the materiality of urban experience, proposing, after Lefebvre, an architecture of events; of **situations**, of momentary ambiance and of everyday life. This constituted a radical shift in the nature of architectural and urban thought, moving it away from its obsession with the object and its geometrical displacements, towards a non-instrumental notion of occupation or inhabitation; away from an idea of use and formal decorum, towards an idea of social occupation and event. This separation was crucial since it extended the scope of architectural production beyond the merely formal, inferring a dynamic opposition in which the terms **object** and **event** were dialectically polarised and through which the term event, retains a conceptual rather than a retinal value. It is this dialectical relationship which makes an event-architecture possible, that is to say, it makes it possible to conceive of an architecture which is not merely formal but which can proceed from notions of social inhabitation and occupation. What made this radical, not to say revolutionary, was that it gave architecture a conceptual dimension, a means of production

Event-Space configurations
for specific Programmes;
Studio Project
Technische Universität,
Berlin, 1996.

beyond the physical construction of buildings. An architecture of event which concentrated on the production of **situations** rather than mute lithic mass, constituted a latent urbanism in which the city could be reconfigured by an act of mind. The programmatic territorialisation of the city could be transformed at will, without construction, as a product of re-occupation, removing any need for the profession of architecture as such. The squat, the street demonstration, the rave, are its legacy.

An architecture of event was no mere figment. Its presence for the S.I. as well as other radical groups of this period was constituted by the impending street revolution and by its eventual precipitation in May '68. Today its presence can be traced within the marginal territories of the modern metropolis, in areas of economic decline and dereliction where established programmes have undergone radical transformations unrestricted by the legal tourniquet of metropolitan and state power.

social teleology of the S.I.'s position. By embracing only the formal implications of an event urbanism, this new pop avant-gardism blindly recuperated the S.I.'s radical politics by forcibly abbreviating their ideas to the impotent terms of an ideology of objects and exchangeable commodities.

What endures of the original political critique of the Situationist International, its political bequest to notions of the contemporary city, must firstly be read through a succession of tawdry recuperations at the hands of a host of reactionary heirs. To all intents and purposes an accurate history of the S.I. is omitted from any pedestrian history of the period; its achievements, although structural to the general development of architectural and urban ideas in the late twentieth century are still considered illegitimate or irrelevant and are absent from the official cultural record. Nevertheless an enduring and latent critique persists within the remaining corpus of the S.I. project.

Event-space configurations, three dimensional models; Studio Project, Technische Universität, Berlin, 1996.

 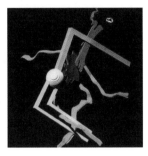

For the Situationist International, placing issues of social occupation at the centre of its urban theory constituted a purposive shift away from the aesthetics of the Corbusian city. Its conceptual re-appropriation of the city as a pregnant geography of fertile 'situations', constructed a radical antithesis to the instrumental formalism of this object based architecture. Once a breach with the object had been made the conceptual transformation of building-use became the tool by which to provide a radical transformation in the programmatics of the city.

At the hands of a contemporaneous and de-politicised avant-garde, to wit Archigram, Haus Rucker, Co-oP Himmel Blau, Super Studio, et al., the S.I.'s protean architecture of events suffered a chic reversal of its political intentions. Although providing the main conduit for a wider dissemination of these ideas, albeit in an altogether adulterated form, this gamut of self-styled poseurs and gallery traders, abandoned the radical

OBJECT/ EVENT

Established architectural sensibility relies upon the notion that spatiality, the **spaceness** of things, is constituted from only one side of the object/event opposition. Although space is commonly held to be a definitive characteristic of architecture, the very stuff of its production, it seems nevertheless to be difficult if not impossible to define. When architects refer to the quality space they do so invariably, as an insinuated quality, as a kind of residuum; as an excess, left over within and between objects. Space from this perspective appears as a quality without substance in the material sense, as a kind of ether which cannot be fashioned **in itself** but must rely for its articulation on the presence and disposition of co-extensive objects. This assumed immateriality of space may be one reason why there is no generic theory of architectural space **sui generis**, which might deal with spaceness explicitly and directly.

are so much metaphysics. From a material perspective, architectural space **in itself** is measurement, a matter of mere metrics.

To conjure up an architecture of pure space is to materialise an abstractis, a quality without content or substance, devoid of any necessary connection to the social body and its cultural dynamics. It is to substantiate what Marxists call a reification, the insinuation of a materiality where no dialectical relationship exists between it and its socio-political context. Notions of architectural space developed in isolation, beyond the influence of social inhabitation, occupation and event, architectures which have often been refered to as **formalist**, are examples of this type of reification. Innocuous, quietist but most importantly de-politicised, they remain devoid of any material contact with the conditions of social reality and are fated to terminate in an architecture of mere objects and impotent commodities.

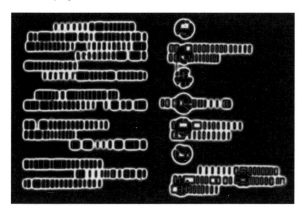

Bar-code choreography for the development of a multi-programmed interior.

Whereas the disposition of objects, the compositional relationship of masses and surfaces, dominates the historical and theoretical perspectives of an official architectural history, topics concerning generic space, the material substance of spatiality, has no apparent presence. Questions concerning the nature of architectural space are questions which avoid the generic issues of space in itself and invariably rest upon something else, some other material aspect of architecture which bears only an extrinsic relationship to it.

Notions of architectural space, such as they are, derive exclusively from geometrical and geographical ideologies which have at their centre, conditions of circumscription, administration, allotment and partition. They belong to a world of metrical division and measurement, closely allied to conditions of jurisdiction, property, ownership and power. Poetic or aesthetic allusions to the generic qualities of architectural space,

An architecture which might embrace the dialectical interchange between measurement and event, however, promises to establish a different ground from which new urban ideas might be fashioned. To propose an approach which attempts a dialectical recuperation of an architecture of mere objects, by challenging it with a material theory of event, would transform its operating context from one of reified space to a socially charged event-space and would, simultaneously, disconnect it from the aesthetic ground it currently occupies by severing its umbilical dependency on the object.

TERRITORIALITY
I devised a number of related projects to examine, in depth, the possibilities of an event based architecture. The first, 'Fragments of Everyday Life', required the production of work which explored the delimitation of the city of Berlin in terms of the territorial zones or fields of everyday use.

These terms attempted to reformulate a spatiality which avoided the strict geometries of the generic European city plan, its squares, streets, loggias, and internal topographies, tracing chronologically interwoven and geographically superimposed territories of social inhabitation occupation and event. The project researched formal vocabularies which articulated a series of **territories** simultaneously occupiable by a variety of programmatic uses.

The term territory proved pivotal to this research. By establishing a counter definition of architectural space based on an analysis of conditions of occupation, the tedious **cliché** of an urban picturesque, the mainstay of establishment urban design, was displaced in favor of an approach which confronted those emerging programmes consequent upon contemporary social, economic and cultural transformations. Among many others the following programmes were identified as symptomatic of the new urban order.

Domestic residential; reflecting a transformation in the nature of marriage and divorce most particularly among the urban middle classes.

Live-work; reflecting the shift into periodic self-employment away from the permanence of jobs for life.

Black economy trading; a feature of the metropolitan periphery and the gradual disintegration of legislative controls over marginal sectors of the economy; the burgeoning **unofficial employment** sector.

Entertainment; occupying a growing and significant part of the waking hours of the **out-of-work**. An industry which has as its most significant by-product the pacification and political emasculation of a disaffected and necessarily alienated section of the metropolitan population.

Leisure; most specifically tourism, now a highly defended territory increasingly subject to draconian policing – the **zero tolerance** policing policies of New York, Los Angeles and more recently London, are examples – in order to sustain the semblance of unruffled decorum within crime riddled metropolitan cores.

Mapped across the city these programmes retained no simple relationship to its overt geometrical plan. The urban and architectural spaces of the contemporary metropolis are subject to conditions of simultaneous inhabitation in which both official and clandestine uses, distinct and contradictory programmes, occupy the same space at different times of the day. The common sense view which architects hold concerning the designation of programme or instrumental use to a geometrical delimitation of the urban mass – as rooms or as city districts – acknowledges only a single

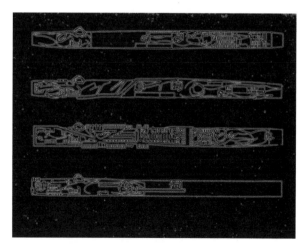

Super-posed programmes within a single building plan.

official designation, a single naming of the use of space. Whereas this may be less significant in terms of mere buildings, where the orchestration of programme is subject more easily to repressive restriction, when it comes to the dynamics of the metropolitan city proper, such a notion is dangerously inaccurate.

For architects urban designing has subliminally retained the structural tautology of Alberti's famous dictum – ...the city is a house; the house is a city. Notwithstanding its recent use as a call to arms by the Neo-rationalist fraternity, it harbors a convenient neo-conservative conceit. The design of buildings and the design of cities, or their parts, must proceed from quite different material contexts and levels of complexity. The house is not a city and the intellectual tools which influence the development of each must necessarily vary to meet the levels of complexity they represent.

Comparisons of **safe**, accessible metropolitan territories, for men, for women and for children, differ greatly as one might expect, but they differ not only topographically but chronologically. There is a palpable contraction of the city, of its accessibility for women and for children at certain times of the day. This familiar example illustrates the dynamics of an urban territoriality no less than it illustrates the compounded ignorance of a profession which has no means of dealing with it.

Evidently some new means of comprehending the contemporary city are needed to confront the following issues;

+ A shift from singular to multiple programmed spaces.
+ The recognition of new and emerging programmes within the metropolitan structure.
+ The establishment of chronological programmatics, examining the territorial occupation of the city at different times.

+ The need to abandon the geometrical picturesque of late modernism, in favour of an event based approach.

LOVE PARADE
In the following project I devised a set of programmes to explore the annual **Love Parade**, Berlin's famous techno-bop cum carnival which takes place in July every year. Subtitled **Event in the extended field** this project was my first attempt to describe a theory of event-architecture.

In order to represent the idea of event, it was necessary to devise a vocabulary of graphical terms which served to describe and to articulate its structure. The parade was assumed to be categorisable as a complex of socially ordered phenomena within a non-geometrical social space. Four main categories were devised. They were as follows:

The cast
a collection of iconographic characters spatially describing specific social actions within the event.

The choreography
a graphical vocabulary describing aspects of the social space of the event as an interaction of cast members.

The territory
the delimitation of discrete social events within the full extent of the event proper.

The field
the full extent of the event.

A MATERIALIST REVISION OF PROGRAMME IN FIELD SPACE
In a number of recent projects concerning the marginal territories of the cities of Paris, Berlin and London, emergent programmes, by which I mean new forms

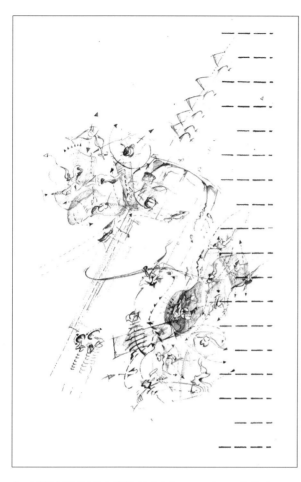

A graphical examination of the spatial choreography created between two adjacent dancing groupes composed of identified cast members, within the love parade crowd.

of inhabitation or building use, were seen to be increasingly common, most especially at the periphery of the metropolitan core, in areas of dereliction and slack legal control. This applied to the housing of non-stable social groups just as much as to improvised sweat-shop premises or illegal traders. The creation of new spatial and programmatic types, which are more market specific, that is to say, more pertinent to the demands created by contemporary socio-demographic changes, is now urgently required in order to confront issues such as the following:

The provision of a sustainable economic and social equilibrium – a **deep** ecological approach – germane to a wider understanding of the complexities of the environment as they affect the metropolitan city. **Urban** contraction of the post-industrial cities of Western Europe and the United States, following the flight of heavy industry to South-East Asia, its replacement with a service based economy and the consequent

re-alignment of their constituent capital territories. **The** lack of appropriate housing provision. Firstly in terms of its distribution within the new capital territories of the post-industrial city and secondly, its inapplicability to emergent social groups and conditions such as:

$+$ single parent families with dependents

$+$ long-term unemployment

$+$ ethnic and social sectarianism

$+$ un-stable family units

$+$ professional inter-city drifters

increased programmatic diversity and complexity precipitated by the fragmentation and transmogrification of established markets under the new conditions of the post-Fordist economic revision.

Antediluvian Urbanism

Any view of what has come to be known as urbanism by Western architects, has to confront from the first, its own view of its origin, no matter how apocryphal or mythical this origin might be. Key aspects of the resident self-image of the Western world, proceed ethnocentrically, not to say divisively from an idolatrous narcissism which pictures itself as an antediluvian Garden of Eden. From this perspective the terms for the production of an effective urbanism, an urbanism which might embrace emerging cultural, economic and political contexts at the end of the twentieth century, and confront the consequences of the much vaunted global market place is always and already contaminated by this insistent archetype. It can be no surprise therefore to find that architectural urbanism, where it has any credence at all, adopts, by default, the revisionism of a medical metaphor by which such an archetype is unremittingly reconstructed through projected acts of prognosis, surgical removal, prosthetic addition and contrived aesthetic healing.

The medical metaphor is neither innocent nor benign here. Incited by an aesthetic addiction to completeness, wholeness, and **Gestalt**, architects conceive the city as a latent pictographic figure always prior to a projected but ultimate consummation. This metaphor masquerading as a altruistic contextualism and as a liberal antidote to the poisonous centralisms of an un-reconstructed Modernism remains well within the intellectual orbit of the Modernist agenda. The very idea that the complexities of the metropolis can be solved by means of a formal revision of its material mass alone and from a single aesthetic perspective, fails to dispense with the preoccupations of what might be called an oppositional Modernism in which a singular vision, a single aesthetic idea, whether stylistically Modernist or not, offers a dogmatically unitarian alternative, a one dimensional urban vision, to solve the ills of the city at a stroke. Singular visions which at present provide the only means to sustain a feeble and thoroughly a-social avant-gardism, such as it remains within the tawdry pages of

Folded intersecting plate configuration, examining the possibilities of superimposed and interweaving programmes within the same continuous space. The floor plate is folded into a flowing topography of sorts upon which the various programmes are displaced. Studio Project Technische Universität, Berlin, 1996. (left and below)

strategies for the production of the contemporary city, will find itself entirely excommunicated from this holy economy.

The territories of the contemporary metropolis are far too dense to be circumscribed by such a contrived commodification, no matter what its constitutive conceptual ground might be. Solutions to contemporary urban problems must be firstly economic and cultural, that is to say political. Traditionally, of course, this has always been the point at which the profession has disconnected itself. By begging professionalism, architecture remains a disinterested service, condemned to merely elaborate rather than influence politically consequent ideas; as such its command of contemporary urban problems remains entirely formal, reductive and one dimensional. If the achievements of a comprehensive post-structuralist critique of Western values is to be taken seriously, that is to say, as effective. And if the political implications of this critique are

indistinguishable trade magazines, also provides the means for a continuous rehabilitation of the indifferent work of the rank and file through an inured and incorporated plagiarism. This is the avant-garde's desperate economy, not to say its implicit Faustian objective. Collage, neo-suprematism, neo-rationalism, deconstruction/ism, fragmentation, complexity, affiliation, folding; are all singular visions of the oppositional type and remain always and already commodities, played as counters in a game of signature and brand peddling.

Within this ideological frame, any material engagement with the terms of urban reality, in its fullest sense, is automatically condemned as of secondary importance with respect to the construction and promotion of a partial, intrinsic and self-referential economy of ideas. Consequently, any urbanism which accepts the structural changes to economic reality at the end of the twentieth century and conceives alternative formal

assumed to be immanent, then notions which repeat the myopic singularities of an oppositional Modernist ideology, medically or otherwise, must be understood as weak at best, not to say entirely misleading; even politically dangerous.

A global economics, surely the precursor of a global mono-culturalism, invites the re-establishment of a unitary Modernism by the back door. If globalism means anything it means oneness, singularity, homogeneity, congruity, sameness. An architectural urbanism which uncritically apes a liberal exegesis on the grounds of taste, thereby ignoring this immanent material reality, most certainly lacks a future and may well constitute the very counter force which will precipitate the permanent shift of urban speculation into other, more apposite spheres of knowledge.

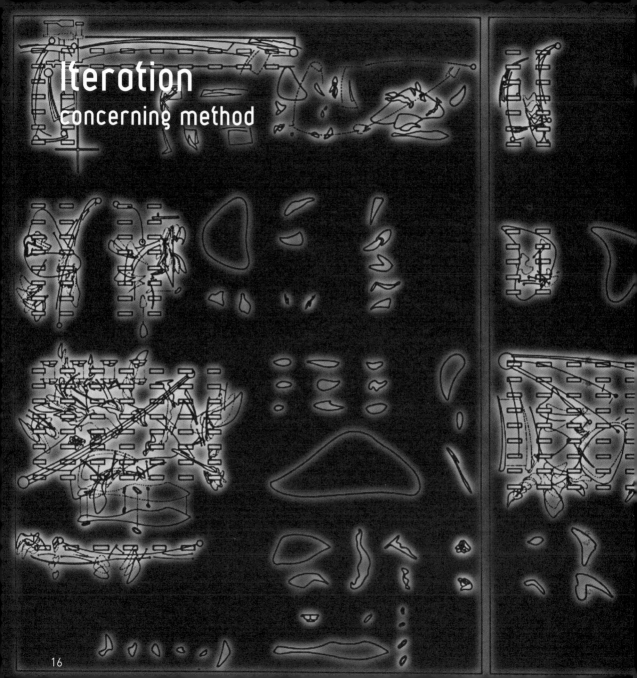

Iteration
concerning method

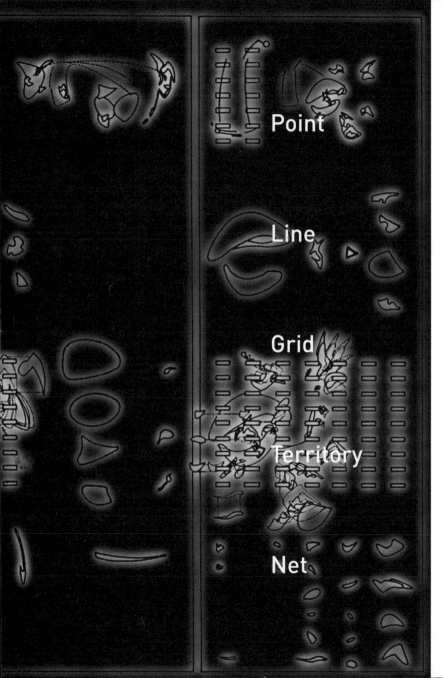

Point

Line

Grid

Territory

Net

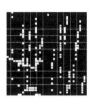

Firstly ITERATION is method.

Why method?

Because I wish to remove myself from this mystical aberration of a post-romantic consciousness, to wit the terminal consciousness of the twentieth century, which has assumed that art and with it what remains of architecture, if anything at all, can be devised by means of some cosmic superstition. That it is a product, in other words, of **IN-spiration**; of the ingestion of an ineffable spirit which supernaturally insinuates production. And, to some degree this would be good enough if, firstly, a God existed which it does not; or secondly that **inspiration** was indeed contaminated with aspects of the supernatural, which it most certainly is not; or thirdly, that this notion of inspiration was anything other than mere social hubris or affectation. Why method? Precisely because it is an abstractis. A machine of abstractions which forces a distance between a normalizing inclination to reproduce aspects of a dominant social taste on the one hand and

a means by which to avoid self-imitation on the other.

Iteration

The iteration is a self-similar but non-identical repetition betraying a drift in form which bears a certain similarity to its origin but which, nevertheless, avoids identity. Iteration is a transformation, under conscious control, moving out from familiar formal territory to the unfamiliar ground of dissimilar invention by means of a series of linked steps. The iteration is a non-identical repetition. A kind of slow transformation in small jumps. And it is precisely the drift in form, which iterative transformation produces, its extenuation of form if you will, which generates the ground for the invention of programme.

Iteration evolved from the indexical method by way of the computer. It is a research tool which generates rather than records formal typologies. As such it was used as the basic tool for the production of work which I have come to refer to as **field studies**.

The main work with this method was undertaken at the Technische Universität Berlin during the winter semester of 1996. A series of five characteristics were isolated as a vehicle for these studies. They were, point, line, grid, territory and net. Each was set within an table or index, (page 20). By utilising the notion of iteration a number of transformations were made by cross referencing each characteristic within the table; hence point to point, point to line, point to grid were compared across the table and so on. At each stage the image changed and by means of a series of retrospective comparisons the table could be composed as a series of necessary and irreducible steps. From an arbitrary origin this method offers an opportunity to exhaust the possible formal expressions of the terms selected.

The results offered a comprehensive vocabulary of formal alternatives which could be further explored by direct application to the pragmatic problem at hand. In each case one term dominates the process of iteration producing a characteristic set of results. In many ways the process is reminiscent of artificial life models, although more complex. Below are some three examples of this method applied to the delimitation of three distinct urban fields. At this level they show only general programmatic organisations but they already offer dramatic alternatives to the formulaic and essentially picturesque urban methods which dominate current architectural practice. This abstract exploration gradually led me to reassess the nature of urban compositional methods and to begin to reformulate a theory which strongly opposed the geometric and figural urban approaches which have dominated the Modernist and Post-Modernist periods alike. Iteration, although ostensibly a formal strategy, aims, ultimately, at programmatic invention and not merely at the production of new forms. The development of alternative formal models makes it possible to research an emergent programmatics by means of systematic post-rationalisation.

The relationship of an iterated formalism to emergent programmes is first of all an open relationship since it encourages the ready invention of new associations and affinities at the level of form. It thereby avoids the hubris of the rational method which insists upon remaining within a closed system, assuming that only questions which are answerable, in their own terms, are worth asking and that the ultimate complexity of issues remains knowable only from within. This refusal of complexity has in recent years become the focus of much new work and thereby much criticism of rational science and its empirical methodology. Emerging initially in the Soviet Union what has come to be known as non-linear geometry or more colloquially, **chaos theory**, has established new terms and techniques for understanding complex systems and complex phenomena.

Iterated matrix. (right)

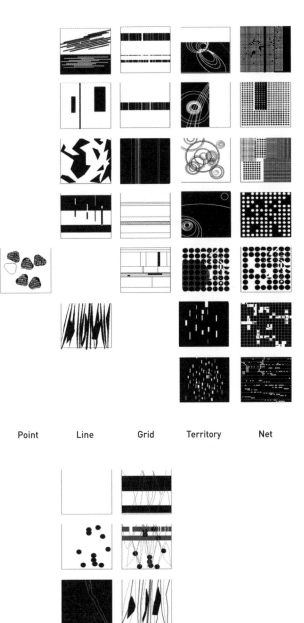

Point	Line	Grid	Territory	Net

	Point	Line	Grid	Territory	Net	
Point						Transformation 1 ....orthogonal Field density...max.
						Transformation 2 ....random Field density...max.
Line						Transformation 3 ....orthogonal Field density...-1
						Transformation 4 ....random Field density...-1
Grid						Transformation 5 ....orthogonal Field density...-2
						Transformation 6 ....random Field density...-2
Territory						Transformation 7 ....orthogonal Field density...-3
						Transformation 8 ....random Field density...-3
Net						Transformation 9 ....orthogonal Field density...-4
						Transformation 10 ....random Field density...-4

Point

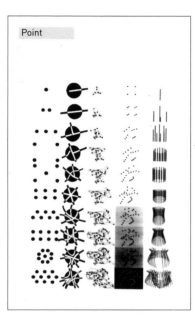

Line

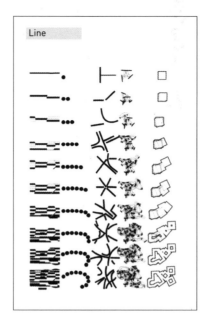

Worked example of the iterated method
by Herbert Klitsch; Studio project
Technische Universität, Berlin, 1997.

Territory

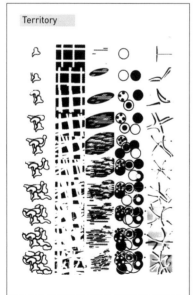

Grid

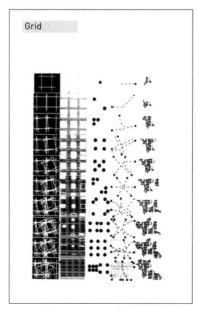

Net

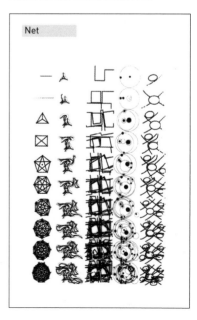

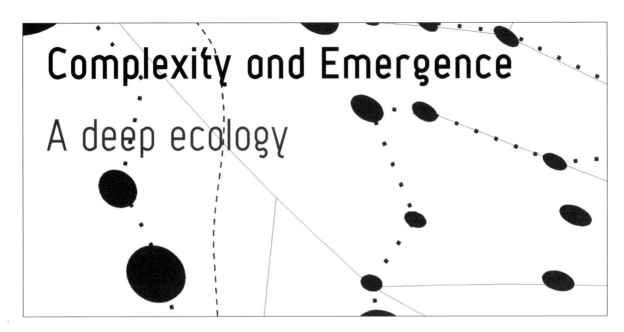

Complexity and Emergence
A deep ecology

Although non-linearity can only provide a formal paradigm for the pursuit of architectural ideas, by doing so it produces a singular opportunity. The pursuit of simplification, a term currently synonymous with elucidation, explanation, definition, interpretation, description, exposition or, most importantly, clarification, is a pursuit for its own sake, and characterises the nature of contemporary praxis both in science and in the practical arts. Indeed, the identification of beauty with methodological simplicity has become a shibboleth of the empirical method. This erstwhile confederation of aesthetics with process, has precipitated a succession of circularities **vis.**

In order to remain within the range of predictability and measurability, only those problems which are, de facto, predictable and measurable should be tackled.
  In order to remain within the realm of the feasible, problems should be restricted in their scope; they should remain practicable and realisable.

The notion of simplicity which might now be associated with its insinuated and sophisticated inference **clarity** in the sense of comprehensibility or explicitness, subtends an ideological figuration upon the discipline which adopts it. Architecture, by applying itself to so called appropriate issues, essentially issues which are intrinsic to its own view of the world, only cramps its already restricted scope. Pragmatism, a predominant belief, dogma even creed of the architectural profession, is a notion moderated by an intrinsic perspective. There are two kinds, at least. The first being short term pragmatism, which tends to myopia, giving itself up to immanent conditions and forsaking long term trends and consequences. The second, long term pragmatism is altogether of a different nature. From this perspective what is pertinent now, may be altogether foolish under different, impending circumstances. This last, long-term pragmatism, is the ecological position. It implies an abrupt reversal, not to say a dramatic expansion

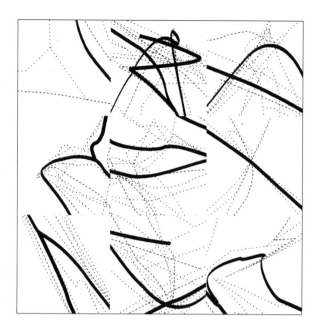

of the profession's current position and sphere of interests, beyond the narrow terms of its own, willfully circumscribed vision.

The city is a deep structure; a dynamic structure. It is complex. This is the rub. This fact leaves the architect, with the intractable problem of how to produce working procedures which can model, more effectively and appropriately, the complex and transforming nature of the contemporary city.

Complex communication net types. (above)

A collection of iterated net models ploting a variety of time/distance relationships for existing and proposed residential communities with densities of less than 10,000 persons per square kilometer and their communications net. Worked examples by Ralph Heckersbruch; studio project Technische Universität, Berlin, 1997. (right)

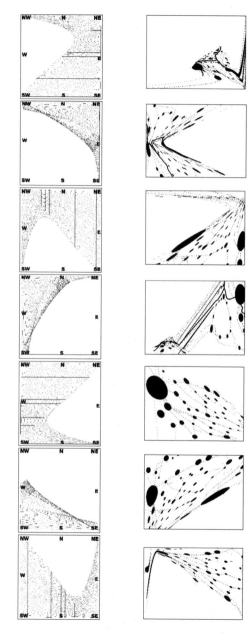

Field Space

concerning phasic, layered, linear, voxelated densities in field space
paradigms of architectural space

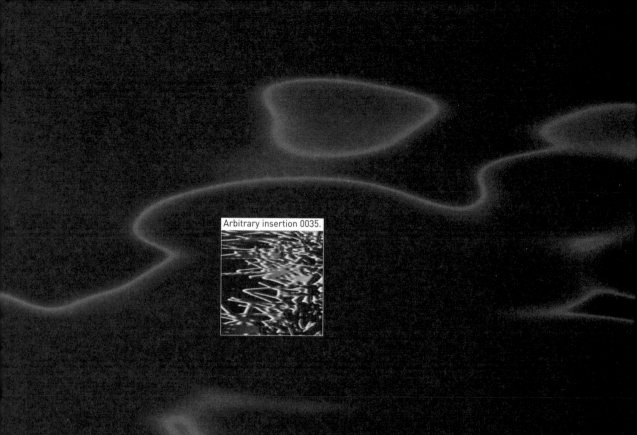

Arbitrary insertion 0035.

concentric, entrained and
five alternative compositional

Glo-goo city.
Arbitrary image No. 1219.

Density

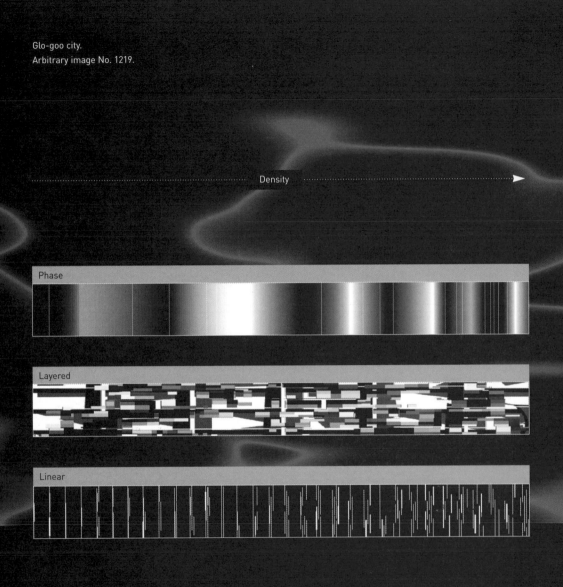

Phase

Layered

Linear

Density

Concentric

Entrained

Voxolated

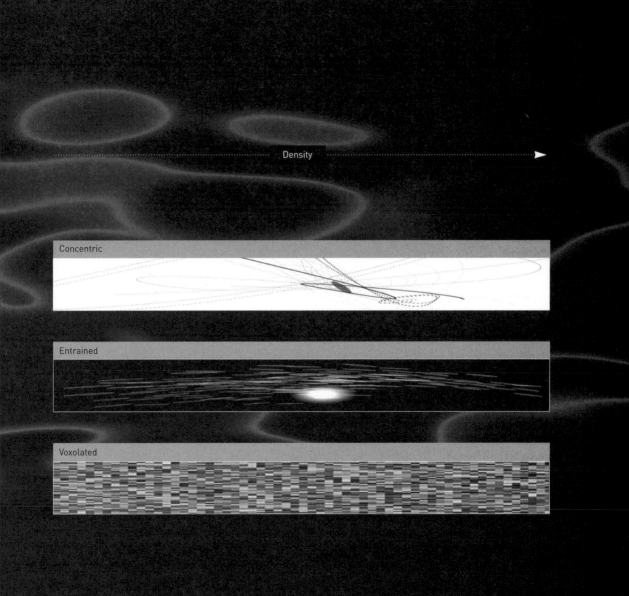

GESTALT

The predominant compositional paradigm of twentieth century Modernism depends upon the association of abstract objects or figures displaced against and contrasted with a neutral, non-figured, **empty** background. It is a play of the presence and absence of graphical objects within the limits of the drawing plane or canvas. A juxtaposition of the configured 'object' constructed in contra-distinction to an undifferentiated and **receding** background. Altogether a process of compositional speculation which has come to be known as the figure/ground, or object/field opposition.

OBJECT is defined as a form, or collection of forms which sustains identifiable figuration in contrast to an undifferentiated, **formless** background. This background, the FIELD, surrounds and delimits distinct objects with a continuous and, most importantly, non-perspectival space. The difference between object and field is one of relative quality and extension.

A field remains a field only insofar as it can be clearly discerned as that which is not the object and **vice-versa**. But within the limits of the drawing plane, objects and fields maintain a degree of interchangeability which is both telescopic and hierarchical, connoting primary, secondary and tertiary stratigraphical levels of complexity. Objects which have significant extensions within a primary field constitute secondary fields when smaller objects are superimposed upon them. They act as fields to these smaller groupings in the same way as the drawing plane constitutes an ultimate field within which the most extended objects of the composition are delineated. Clearly this hierarchical interchange is infinitely extendible.

SPACE

Two versions of the object/field compositional method have prevailed. **Superimposition** – the super-position of transparent or partly transparent figures to form complex layered objects. And **Collage** – the association and juxtaposition of disparate elements from a variety of unrelated contexts to form complex layered objects. They remain contemporaneously the only methods used in architectural composition by the establishment and by the **avant-garde** alike.

One must be careful here to separate the phenomenological aspects of spatial experiences and their subsequent appearance in architecture. **Raumfindung** or 'felt-space', is contingent upon physical occupation; of being present in space. **This is not the experience of the designing architect.** Architecture is firstly drawing and the architectural drawing affords merely an analogy of felt space. Consequently, there can be no production of a generic space, **per se**. The architectural drawing yields only specific spaces, achieved by insinuation, through the juxtaposition, delimitation and layering of graphical surfaces and solids. What is called **space** for the designing architect holds no palpable generic meaning in itself. It is a product of the extrinsic affinity of two dimensional objects in relational fields.

More interestingly, however, both superimposition and collage remain primarily figural approaches, privileging the object pole of the object/field opposition. Although **Gestalt** theory relies upon the contingency of the figure/ground, object/field relationship, in architecture only figuration, the comparative articulation of objects, retains any palpability. Architecture is primarily a game of objects, their relational ground, **the field**, is conventionally discounted as the un-theorised category **space**. And although habitually referred to as the **modus operandi** of architectural production, 'space', **per se**, remains effectively an indistinct, residual quality, without material substance or determinable form.

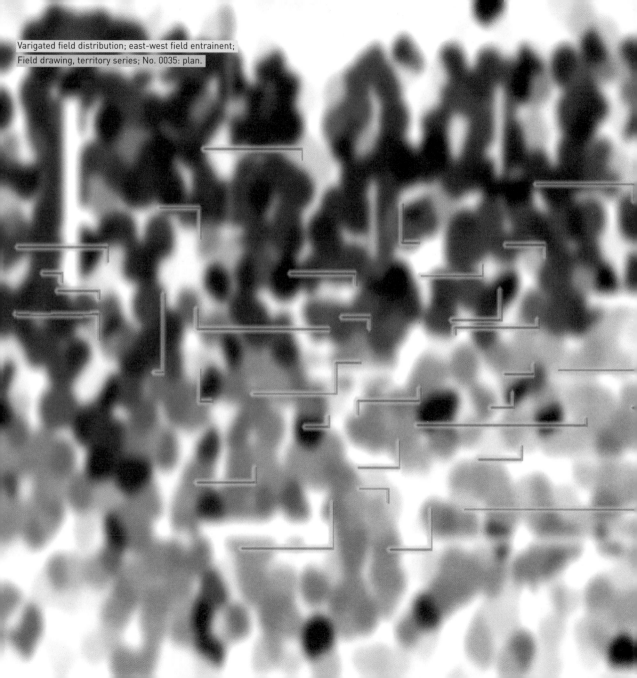

Varigated field distribution; east-west field entrainent;
Field drawing, territory series; No. 0035: plan.

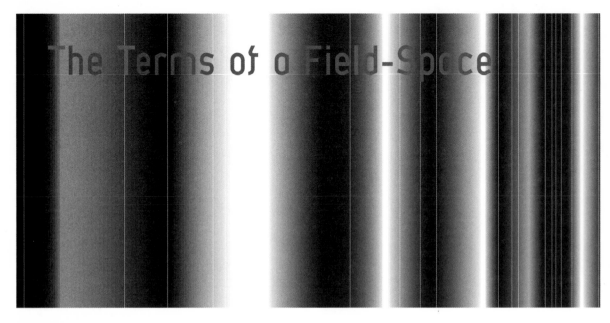

A question now suggests itself; **vis. is it possible to invert this obsession for objects and objectness and attempt to establish an architecture which proceeds from the field pole of object/field opposition?**

SUPREMATISM

In the Suprematist scheme space is insinuated rather than illustrated. It is a function of an implied reading of the canvas it is not **literally** depicted in the manner of, say, a measured perspective. Depth is connoted by the use of an optical illusion. The formal tropes of superimposition, relative size and colour saturation affect the displacement of pictorial figures producing a sensation of depth. Lacking the implied perspectival geometries of cone of vision, horizon and vanishing point, the constituent figures appear to float freely within an infinitely extendible space which expands as it moves back from the plane of vision. Suprematist pictorial frames do not compress the view like a window might. Neither do they position nor direct the

viewer. Within them space is isotropical, that is to say, it is effectively measureless; an extensive continuum. Such frames cut the connoted space arbitrarily. Suprematist objects are consequently scaleless and their field of spatial extension is limitless.

WEATHER MAP

Einstein's unified field theory lends itself usefully as a descriptive analogy with regard to the Suprematist project. Here matter which is assumed to inhere ubiquitously in space, identifies itself as fields of relative density or high pressure. Space and object are considered to be made of the same stuff, distinguishable by their relative densities alone. Within the Suprematist scheme the distribution of formal values, the relationship between figure and ground, resembles this description, rather like a weather map (opposite) with colour fields denoting zones of relative pressure. Space and plane, object and field can now be interpreted as equivalent

Field densities/Pressure map.

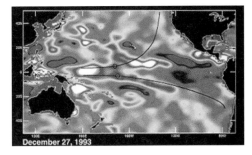

December 27, 1993

Pressure distribution Pacific Ocean.

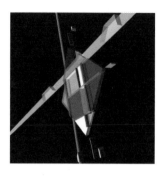

materialities. Usefully this analogy provides a means by which the object/field opposition can be related as a continuum. High pressure denoting objectness, low pressure denoting fieldness etc.

IDENTITY

Suprematist compositional procedures discarded conventional notions of pictorial identity, the spatial positioning of objects within a virtual yet measurable space. In the work illustrated here (opposite) the juxtaposition of the constituent compositional objects are displaced against a receding, undifferentiated white field – the plane of the canvas. Two readings can be made of this composition.

The first perceives these objects as a pictorial figure, opposing the flat background of the canvas. The second, conceives this flat plane as an extensive void within which the fragments are scattered. When one perceives the canvas as flat, objects insinuate a measured, relational space in the

perspective sense; as if they are seen from above as in a plan view, or from the side as in elevation. The relational field maintains only a nominal value. When the canvas is conceived to extend beyond the clustered fragments, the relational field acquires a dynamism which forces the fragments to oscillate perceptually, giving a palpable experience of a spatialised field. This is the experience of FIELD SPACE.

EXTENSION

The neo-plastic, de-Stijl canvases of Piet Mondrian, particularly the Diamond Series, provide a second example of the field space experience (above). Depth, in the sense of relative position, is denoted by the differences in colour saturation and adjacent contrasts between the various objects which constitute the full composition. But such coloured objects are not entirely contiguous. They are divided by a grid of lines in black, a tonal value denoting recession. Mondrian's famous complaints at the Witney

'Eight red rectangles';
Kasimir Malevich.

Assumed projection
of the solids into three
dimensional space.

Assumed projection
of the solids into three
dimensional space.

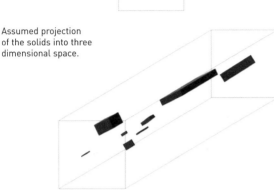

concerning the framing of his canvases were concerned with the way these lines were to be conceived of by the viewer. He didn't want them to be visually obstructed by a conventional picture frame since he had conceived them as part of a continuous grid encircling the earth. A field net of sorts, of which the canvas was a mere record, as if it had been held up to this grid to be stamped with its impression. The presence of these lines and their insinuated extensions, implies the presence of a conceptual field, a deep space in which the colour objects now appear to float. This is the experience of FIELD SPACE.

DYNAMIC EQUILIBRIUM

Above right and lower left show a notional interpretation of a Kazimir Malevich canvas **Eight Red Rectangles**, 1915, in order to illustrate the potential extension of the insinuated field. By making a reading in which the canvas denotes an extensive void of space receding from the picture plane, it is possible to interpret the

displacement of the object fragments as extended and scattered within a projected rectangle. The possible extension of the relational field and the masses of the fragmented objects within it, their various juxtapositions etc., remains ultimately indeterminate. Consequently a number of potential readings, that is to say the number of latent reconfigurations of the constituent elements within an extended space is provoked by the work. This is the experience of FIELD SPACE.

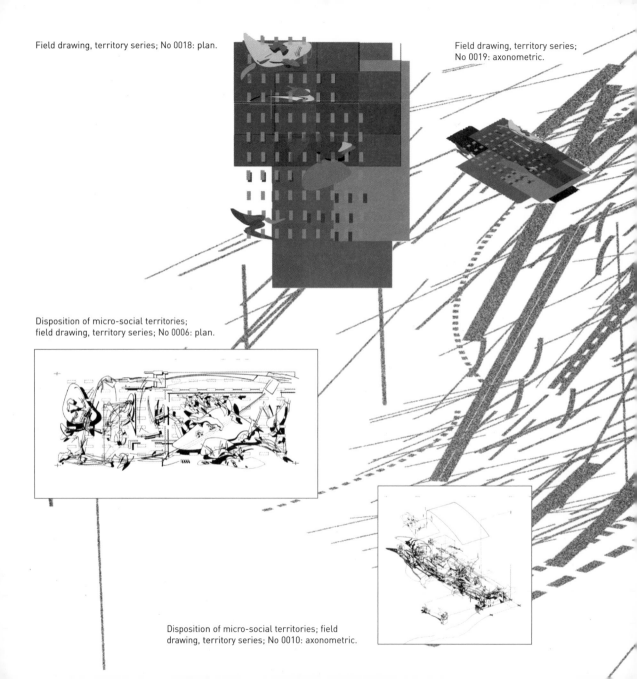

Field drawing, territory series; No 0018: plan.

Field drawing, territory series;
No 0019: axonometric.

Disposition of micro-social territories;
field drawing, territory series; No 0006: plan.

Disposition of micro-social territories; field
drawing, territory series; No 0010: axonometric.

Fragmented linear field; plan installation,
Technische Universität, Berlin, 1996.

Dynamic field fragmentation; installation,
Technische Universität, Berlin, 1996.

Fragmented linear field; elevation
instalation, Technische Universität, Berlin, 1996.

territorial fragmentation

East Europe
the new situation

When the ideology of the figural
object replaced its close ally,
the ideology of figural space,
the effective, political experience
of the city failed to change at
all — in the contemporary city
bourgeois values remain intact.

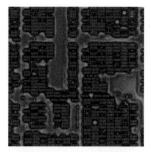
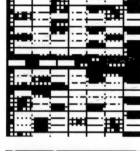
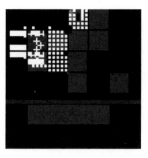
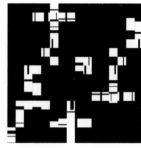

Various iterations of city density models with alternative density and phased space distributions. These models are compiled as a series of typological alternatives for the distribution of simple graphical masses – 1x1, 1x2, 1x3 and 1x4 – rectangles to explore the possibilities of a field distribution of spaces on a square grid.

THE VIENNA BRATISLAVA CONNECTOR

The legacy of the European city maintains a dysfunctional division between the subsectors of its Modernist revision. Housing, industry, office and shopping remain discontiguous and separated. An overprovision of redundant commercial office space is, for example, juxtaposed to a severe underprovision of appropriate housing stock. A structural characteristic of commercially driven development and piecemeal planning policy. The strict zoning divisions maintained between these ostensibly different building types exacerbates the dysfunctionality of the contemporary city by excluding the possibility of the superimposition of uses.

If we are to believe those who suggest that capitalism has once again revised itself into a more fragmented, plural, **post-Fordist** structure, then the traditional structure of the city mass, its inflexible zoning policies, may prove ineffective to control the progressive fragmentation and pluralism of what now might be called the post-Fordist city.

There is an internal contradiction inherent to bourgeois views of the contemporary city. The demands of post-Fordist economies on the urban mass require a flexibility in its structure which runs counter to the inertia projected on significant urban restructuring by bourgeois taste. Indeed, it is now politically unlikely that significant urban restructuring can take place in the foreseeable future in any major West-European city at a point in time when, changes to their economic and social structures have rendered traditional building types inflexible.

The transmogrification of urban and regional fields in line with the new realities of post-Fordist economic life may nevertheless establish themselves in regions peripheral to the major metropolitan centres of the West-European economic theater. For the major cities

Vienna+Bratislava linear connector

of the former East Block, economic modernisation renders comprehensive urban restructuring much more likely in the short term. It is in this region, rather than within the wealthier cities of the EU that the first material response to post-Fordist economic conditions will be seen.

Several cities have now become the focus of this change in economic perspective, they are among others: Berlin, Leipzig, Dresden, Prague, Bratislava, Vienna, Warsaw, Budapest, Lublijana, Sarajevo, Belgrade,Tirana, Sofia and Bucharest.

These cities, situated on Europe's Eastern flank, maintain developed urban infra-structures, pools of skilled labour and a university educated professional class. Population pressure on these Eastern cities is projected to mount. The introduction of post-Fordist production, characterised by a shift away from heavy industry to light industrial assembly, to soft production

and to service economy markets, will constitute structural changes in the nature of regional redevelopment.

These resources promise to constitute a phalanx of market opportunities to accommodate the inevitable Eastern expansion of the West-European cultural block through Germany. The region has the potential to develop a linear structure of inter-connected trading centres on the Eastern edge of a greater European market. Within this emerging region four inter-regional territories of special interest and immediate economic potential, suggest themselves as worthy of detailed study. These are as follows:-

+ the Berlin, Leipzig, Dresden trading triangle
+ the inter-urban plane connecting Vienna and Bratislava;
+ the Bulgarian-Albanian, Black Sea coastal strip;
+ the territories to the East affected by the air

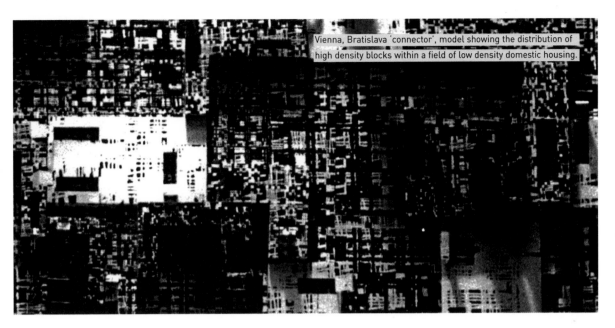

Vienna, Bratislava 'connector', model showing the distribution of high density blocks within a field of low density domestic housing.

corridor network linking the principal airports of the European Union with those of the former East Block.

The Vienna-Bratislava linear connector project undertaken at the Technische Universität Berlin in the winter of '96 was planned as the first of four studies examining these issues. It concentrated on examining the drift of urban re-development in this Eastern sector of the greater European theater.

Its principle points of engagement were as follows:

+ the impact of Eastern European involvement in the trading markets of the West;
+ the availability of **cheap** land, within this Eastern sector;
+ the presence of a skilled service class;
+ the possibility for the seeding of a large purchasing base for retail and service markets;
+ the presence of a small but mobile multi-lingual professional class;

+ the slow but inevitable emergence of a bourgeois class;
+ the inevitable shift away from heavy industry to service based economies;
+ the reduction in time/distance relationships between the various cities of the region;
+ the establishment of an ecologically stable population.

ECOLOGY

The precipitant growth of the world's largest cities is set to decline even as the world's total population increases. The phenomenon of rapid urbanisation, perforce of its consequent social transformations, places a break on population relative to non-urban growth rates. Information from the World Heath Organisation and the World Bank has suggested recently that the total size of city populations may bear some relation to social praxis. Most significantly, cities which have populations in excess of three million tend to establish the social conditions which facilitate declining population increases. This is a phenomenon which seems to indicate that the mores of the metropolitan city might lead, albeit indirectly, to positive ecological consequences.

Within the next thirty years the majority of the world's metropoli will be growing at decreased and decreasing rates. However, this does not mean, in the short term

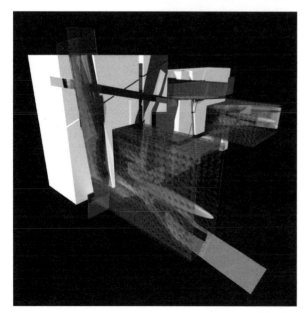

Multi-programmed block.
Aerial perspective. (right)
General perspective. (below)

at least, that this situation will effect a declining global population. There will be many more metropolitan cities around the world as smaller urban structures experience rapid urbanisation. Indeed, this phenomenon is set to transmute as adjacent metropoli or medium sized cities of three to five million coalesce into extended urbanised zones or urban fields – an urban form known, in its most extensive condition, as the **megalopolis**, already established on the Western seaboard of the United States and observable, in Western Europe, within the river valleys of the Schelde, Meuse and Rhine.

Vienna-Bratislava was chosen as the most likely site of an extensive metropolitan field. The existing economic discrepancy between these two adjacent city populations was taken as a paradigm for the development of a series of ideas concerning the creation of an extended urban field as a linking connector.

THE CONNECTOR

The Vienna-Bratislava connector proposed a comprehensive mass redevelopment of the region flanking the Danube between the two cities. The proposal was for an extended low-rise housing zone with associated mid- to high-rise infrastuctural facilities linking the two cities across the flood plain of the Danube, thereby constituting a continuous Vienna-Bratislava urban mass with a population in excess of 8 million.

Operating a field strategy the project proposed a series of mid-rise, deep plan blocks with an average size of some 100,000 m². These were situated within a undifferentiated ground of non-planned **wild housing**. These multi-programmed facilities containing commercial shopping, office, light-industrial, housing, parking and leisure facilities, at densities of 15,000 inhabitants per square kilometer, were positioned within the intra-urban zone as a series of condensers,

Typology of alternative programmatic distributions within the high density multi-programmed blocks.

Iteration 11/3

Iteration 12/1

Iteration 15/9

Iteration 16/21

periodically focusing the surrounding low-rise housing, at 2,000–4,000 inhabitants per hectare. They constituted a series of nodes or fixed points within the extended urban mass.

Two aspects of this approach are worth elaborating. First, the strategic planning of the multi-programmed block was conceived as a transformation of the multi-centered urban model reminiscent of Los Angeles or Houston, but at much higher densities. The condenser block, applied the idea of the Constructivist social condenser, to commercial requirements, focusing shopping, office and institutional facilities into one built mass. Rather like a citadel the block stands isolated within a surrounding screed of unplanned housing. Secondly that the surrounding housing adopted the precedent of what has come to be known in central Europe as **wild housing**. A phenomenon entirely absent from the highly controlled urban environments typical of the E.U. and North America,

wild housing is a prominent feature of the contemporary urban expansion of several former East-Block cities, most significantly Sarajevo and Belgrade. Neither barriado nor shanty town it is an uncontrolled, unplanned development type for the new central European urban middle class. Built professionally but outside the legal strictures regulating such development in the West, it is formally chaotic yet functionally organic, producing a series of emergent programmatic relationships and a dramatically different spatial quality.

Field matrix density study; iteration 165.

Field matrix density study; iteration 182.

Field matrix density study; iteration 207.

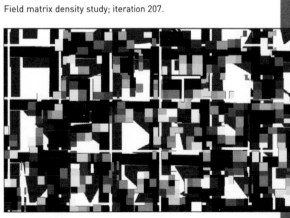

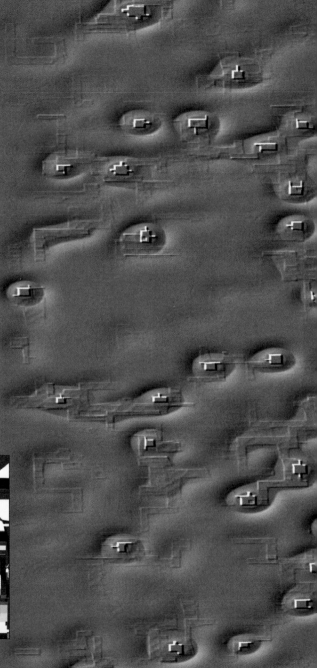

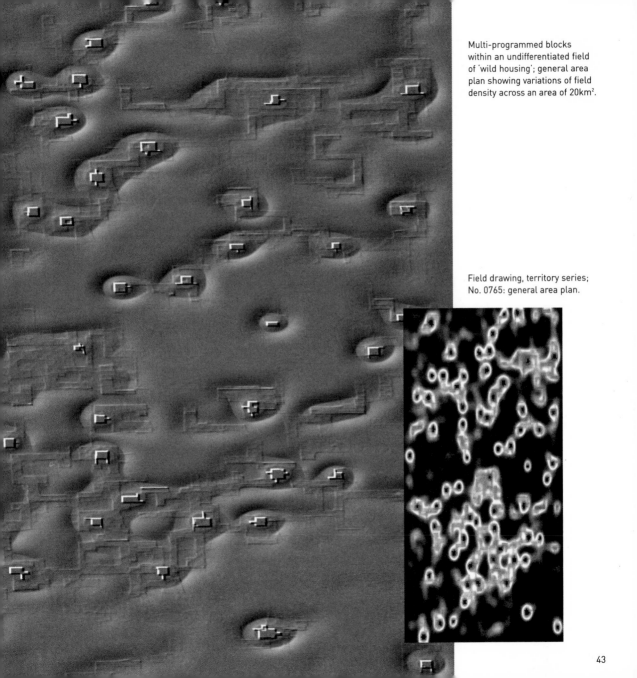

Multi-programmed blocks within an undifferentiated field of 'wild housing'; general area plan showing variations of field density across an area of 20km².

Field drawing, territory series; No. 0765: general area plan.

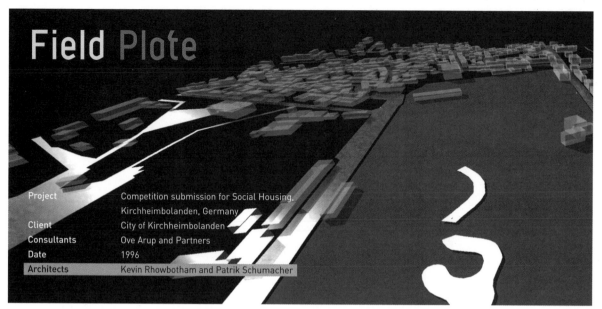

Field Plote

Project	Competition submission for Social Housing, Kirchheimbolanden, Germany
Client	City of Kirchheimbolanden
Consultants	Ove Arup and Partners
Date	1996
Architects	Kevin Rhowbotham and Patrik Schumacher

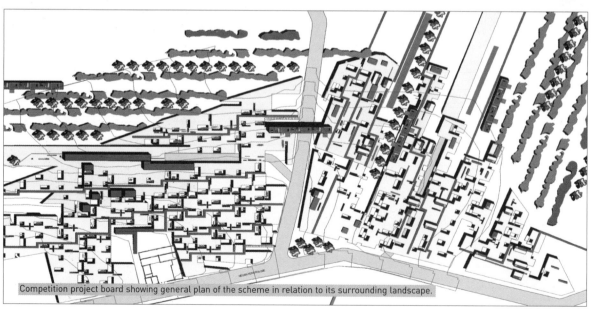

Competition project board showing general plan of the scheme in relation to its surrounding landscape.

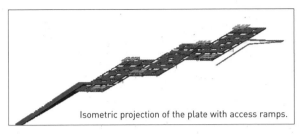
Isometric projection of the plate with access ramps.

Figure-ground drawing of the plate showing courtyards, access staircases and site ramps to the north and west.

The competition required a high density housing scheme for a sensitive, green field site adjacent to the historic town of Kirchheimbolanden near Munich, South Germany. It called for a low impact intervention catering for both able-bodied and disabled inhabitants at commercially effective densities, whilst maintaining views from the old town to the open fields behind the project site.

To achieve the highest densities without a high-rise solution we adopted a cluster housing paradigm, following closely the theories of the structuralists, but most especially the Smithson's 'Mat Building' thesis of the 1970s and the anthropological concerns of Aldo Van Eyke. The project was designed as a continuous plate, gently curving to the North of the site. This plate, highly insulated and landscaped, constituted a datum above and below which disabled and able dwelling units were distributed respectively. The key idea was to place the disabled dwellings

– 15% of the total – above the plate facilitating ease of movement. Dwellings for the able-bodied were placed below the plate and could be entered by means of a shared staircase, terminating in an open court. The top of the plate was cut to facilitate the penetration of natural day-lighting to all light-seeking rooms and to provide external space to meet the stringent German social housing standards. Car-parking was situated beneath the two main site ramps which connected the plate with the surrounding site.

The result was a low rise hill of sorts, invisible from the existing village of Kirchheimbolanden save for the few single story structures or second story additions to below plate dwellings which appeared as a series of scattered fragments in a landscaped field. The design proved innovative insofar as it achieved higher densities than conventional social housing types at reduced cost providing, in addition, considerable traffic free social space at close proximity to each domicile.

The form of the project emerged from a strategic, not to say politically motivated return to a strictly material framework for the production of space, which concentrated on programmatic solutions as the principle ground for a revitalised engagement with the design problem.

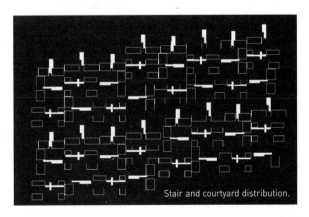
Stair and courtyard distribution.

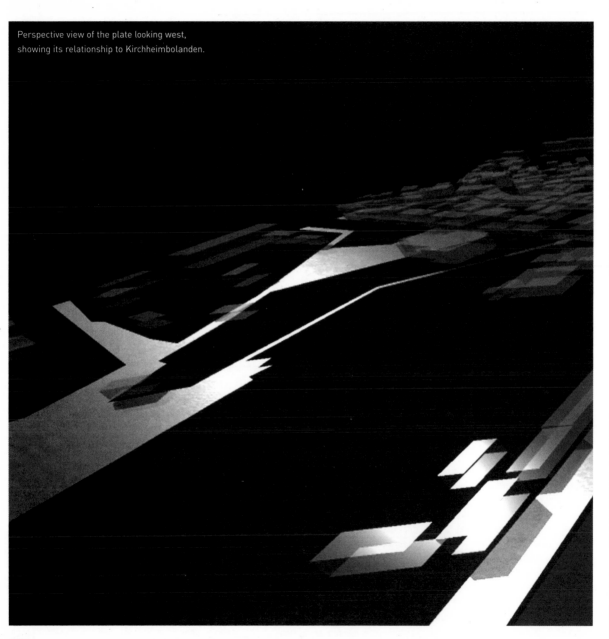

Perspective view of the plate looking west,
showing its relationship to Kirchheimbolanden.

Model of the cut plate.

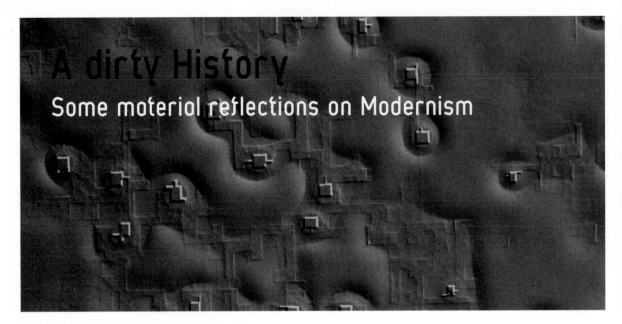

A dirty History
Some material reflections on Modernism

The Fordist phase of twentieth century capitalism fragmented the territories of the neo-classical city more comprehensively than those parallel changes in the vocabulary of architecture, erroneously termed **Modernism**. Indeed it was this very transformation in the economic base which fostered the material context of Modernism proper and not the other way around.

All talk of **Zeitgeist** in this regard smacks of recuperation and collusion. The **spirit** of the Modernist transformation of aesthetic taste was cast by the material context of a Fordist economic revision – precisely by a shift from artisanal to mass production – and not by the inventive genius of a section of the European bourgeoisie, be they artists or businessmen. Historians and critics of the period confounded the material transformations of architecture as the product of inspirational genius and not as the superstructural adaptation of a social class to the new realities of Fordist mass production.

The instrumentality of the plan, inherited from nineteenth-century commercial functionalism, was ideologised by the Modernist avant-garde as a recuperating tactic, alloying the venal demands of commercial development with high-brow bourgeois taste. NEUE SACHLICHKEIT, (new realism), marks a place, at least for those critics who were to valorise Modernism, of a spectacular intellectual conceit which transformed an aesthetics of sheer economic necessity, into one which maintained the hubris of social distinction through high art. The rough trading of a new economic context which precipitated a viscous spiral of competitive cost cutting and a consequent transformation of building practices required a strategic recuperation of the values of mass production in line with the natural conservatism of bourgeois taste. Neue Sachlichkeit provided the heroic shibboleth not to say the moral tourniquet with which to check the flow of a now unfashionable and, at least, un-Modern cultivation for the decorated, the sentimental and the familiar.

The metaphor of the machine reified this shift in taste. The machine aesthetic, a term which secures meaning only at the broadest level of comparison, is charged primarily with a reformist morality of the evangelical variety. This is its primary political tactic, devised to secure the acquiescence of a skeptical bourgeoisie for the cruder exigencies of the new Fordist economics. The machine, or more precisely MACHINE-ISM, became and still remains to architects among many others, the epistemological paradigm par-excellence which drives an acceptance of all things machine like – produced by the machine. At the level of aesthetics, and by an inevitable implication by politics also, this is a dangerous moment, since the alienating exigencies of Fordist mass production are subject to a recuperative and propagandist revision in the name of high art, thereby dissolving the ground of any counter-critique.

The heroic Modernist avant-garde perceived an

opportunity for self advancement within the burgeoning territories of international cultural notoriety, by exploiting a disconcerting aesthetic. In the social style of post-First World War descent, it expropriated the mantle of the renegade artist whilst providing the reforming building industry and its capitalists with precisely what they wanted. The result was White-Style Modernism; an affected revision of stripped classicism with neo-plastic overtones.

The corpus of Modernism has offered little in terms of any direct programmatic invention, other than the free plan which by definition avoids social and programmatic specificity. It was unable to devise a programmatics which constituted a fundamental critique of the nature of inhabitation. Bourgeois mores were assumed as natural and normal and remained the principle guiding paradigm for Modernist production.

Of paramount importance to a contemporary conception of the metropolis and its subsequent revisions under the terms of corporate and post-Fordist capitalism, was the utopian/distopian **Ville Radieuse** tendency, initiated journalistically by the neo-Nietzschean Charles Jeanerette. Without a hint of irony the modern bourgeois city was eulogised as the master machine, conflating authoritarianism with liberal sectarianism. In line with Ford's venal interpretation of mechanism the city became zonally dismembered into exclusive instrumental territories like a geographical production line. The subsequent transformations of capitalism have since rendered this dismemberment altogether dysfunctional. But the insistent grip of the Corbusian city on the sensibilities of contemporary architects, most particularly its picturesque formalism, persists nevertheless.

The products of Modernism proper, such as they were, and certainly those of its heroic tendency, were so thin

on the ground as to have little impact on public consciousness. Mass publication inadvertently rendered them significant commodities, whilst appropriating a parental Modernism as the shibboleth of an emergent life-style culture. Contrary to the fraudulent mantras of official architectural history, Modernism was re-animated by a populist Frankenstein, journalism, and by this self-interested phenomenon alone. It was not, of itself, significant.

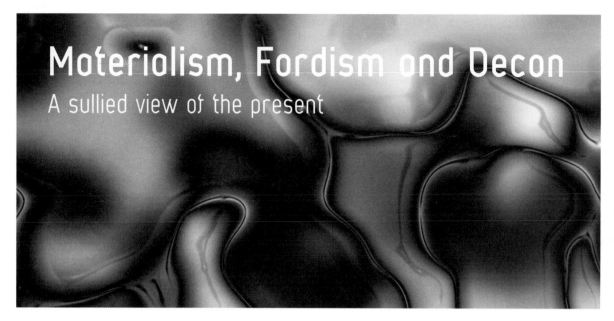

Materialism, Fordism and Decon
A sullied view of the present

DEATH OF COMMUNISM (Augenblick)

COMMUNISM is the exasperation of the bureaucratic cancer that has always wasted humanity. A German cancer, a product of the characteristic German preparationism. Every pedantic preparation is anti-human and wearies fortune. History, life and the earth belong to the improvisers. — Also sprach Marinetti

It is a common opinion today that communism in the sense of the Marxist philosophical project, its antecedents and its precedents, has universally failed to establish the political terms of its continuing survival. That it has died a **death** of sorts, signified dramatically by the implosion of the East Block and that its necessary, not to say natural successor, is the so called liberal politics of market capitalism. That society as a comprehensible object and as a phenomenon of human social existence has somehow given up its cohesive forces and become fragmented, non-functioning and redundant. That the nature of

human groups, should they exist at all, have, somehow, matured through this period of naive social community to be reborn as a fragmented collection of ever more independent individuals, psychologically isolated, yet consciously social in the pro-active sense of an ingenuous managerial administration. That is, in the sense of a networking but atomised quasi-community of individuals.

Born of the radicalism of the 1960s, the last social uprisings in the West, and prior to the so called **velvet revolutions** which witnessed the transformation of the former state capitalist economies of the East Block, an atomising and fragmenting tendency established itself within the social body of everyday life. By common consent, Communism, such as it remained at the end of the 80s, was finally and irredeemably dead. An extension of the autonomy of the self within the structure of a market economy had defeated its communist adversary, by a natural revolution of the historical and social wheel. The naturalness of this irreversible and providential transformation has been absolutely assumed. Communism is now seen as a pre-existing and, in a very real sense, an antecedent structure, something we have finally out-grown.

It would be hard to deny that there has been a profound sea change in the nature of Western culture since the end of the second world war. Emerging with the post-war Beat generation as an echo of the anti-bourgeois sentiments of a renegade pre-war avant-garde, of DADA, of Surrealism, and focused upon the incomplete project of social communism, a new and palpable sensibility appeared towards the end of the 60s, precipitated by the social and political context of the 68 protests. New ideas of independence fostered a certain social fragmentation, which engendered, in turn, the creation of new oppositional and anti-establishment social groups operating outside universally accepted social norms.

NARCISSISM AND THE SOCIAL SELF (Geselligkeit)
Perhaps Dylan's prophetic phrase *"... **your sons and your daughters are beyond your command...**"* signifies the impending breach. Although famously eschewed, with some hindsight, as merely a temporary phase of a maturing and currently incumbent, liberal middle class, it portends, not a revolution by force or descent which it seemed to imply at the time, but rather the formation of a new narcissistic self, the occupant of an atomised and fragmented social world in which all material possibilities are simultaneously available; a world in which the satisfaction of these desires leads only to the perpetual generation of others. It insinuates in the strongest terms the final and decisive arrival of the Nietzschean nomad, a veritable Duc Jean Floressas des Esseintes of Huysmans prophetic novel 'Á Rebours' and of Oscar Wild's 'Dorian Gray'. Neurotic, unsatisfiable, unfulfillable and restless.

Hey there people I'm bobby brown:
They say I'm the cutest boy in town.
My car is fast, my teeth is shinny:
I tell all the girls they can kiss my heinie

Here I am at a famous school:
I'm dressing sharp, I'm acting cool
I got a cheer leader here wants to help with my paper:
Let her do all the work 'n maybe later I'll rape her

Oh God I am the american dream:
I do not think I'm too extreme
I'm a handsome sonofabitch:
Gonna get a good job and be real rich.

— Frank Zappa 'The American Dream'

This is a narcissism which is very difficult to speak of in any transparent sense today, since it is now internalised within the consciousness of Western culture and has come to be accepted as the ultimate, and in many ways, the terminating paradigm of an intrinsic consciousness at the end of the twentieth-century. The so called **ME** decade of the 80s, re-invigorated and focused the expansion of social narcissism giving it a clear political thrust and moral exoneration. The much vaunted **end of communism** personified this complexity of intentions in the figures of Ronald Regan and Margaret Thatcher and reified it as the yuppie revolution. The notion of a social body was disfigured, not withstanding the **de facto** evidence of everyday life, to a point at which a British Prime Minister could unselfconsciously declare that there was "... no such thing as society, just a collection of individuals".

Bearing considerably upon the philosophical inclinations of the late nineteenth-century philosopher Friederich Nietzsche a nihilistic anti-social individualism found increasing acceptance most significantly among the urban middle class. For example, the eminent sociologist Georgi Simmel makes the following observation...

> The atrophy of individual culture through the hypertrophy of objective culture is one reason for the bitter hatred which the preachers of the most extreme individualism, above all Nietzsche, harbor against the metropolis. But it is, indeed, also a reason why these preachers are so passionately loved in the metropolis and why they appear to the metropolitan man as the prophets and saviors of his most unsatisfied yearnings.

Nietzsche's central philosophical tenet eschews hidden content of any kind, most particularly of the Kantian variety, making appearance and not substance the corner stone of its philosophical drive, affirming, as it does so, the absence of any reality beneath the surface of things. This philosophical trajectory has assumed gigantic proportions in the hands of neo-Nietzscheans such as Jean Baudrillard, for example, who portrays the world as a play of hyper-real images and as a regressive chain of floating representations without source. Representations which are themselves representations in turn, irrevocably torn from their signifying origin.

The urbanist and social critic Richard Sennett sets the phenomenon of the narcissistic self into a broader historical perspective. Narcissism, Sennett argues has come about due to the erosion of public life since the end of the nineteenth-century from four directions. Paraphrased they are as follows:

Changes in the ideas of private and public space since the great revolutions at the end of the eighteenth-century, most particularly within an emergent bourgeois class.

Nineteenth-century bourgeois privatisation and the consequent fragmentation of the social mass as it became a primarily urban rather than agrarian population.

The fragmentation of extended family structures with the increasing industrialisation of the urban mass. The emergence of the nuclear family and with it a new psychology (Simmel) of the exclusive family atom as a defense against the terrors of an increasingly destabilised and destabilising society and economy.

The universal acceptance of the terms of an exchange economy dependent upon the dematerialisation of all value into the terms of money trading. In this system enduring values were replaced by a code of immanence according to which the immediacy, the brute fact of things, was taken as the irreducible ground of reality in and of itself.

Narcissistic individualism may have been prepared by the contexts Sennett describes but it garnered its enduring psychological force from the internalisation of the Nietzschean philosophical agenda. From this perspective reality is as it appears at the surface, the undeniable fact of things. Denying the possibility of enduring values it proposes a stark philosophy of appearances. Reality is for Nietzsche, as it was to become for the major philosophical interests of the late twentieth-century, primarily an aesthetic category.

The dislocation of self from the social body is manifest most dramatically in the arts, where the disingenuous image of the heroic Faustian Modernist, as lone adventurer, has presided over the general ideological frame of production. The disappointment of the social ambitions of the Modernist project, engendered a slow disintegration and final amelioration of the erstwhile social commitment of the architectural profession, most especially at its avant-gardist margins. The consequences of this for architecture as a social project and as a political player, within a general discourse of social critique and cultural production, were not merely significant, but latently terminal.

In tandem with the rise of a social narcissism, a new economic territory was being drawn out, which revised the conditions of capital production throughout the West. Building upon the radical changes wrought by the Second World War an entirely unprecedented economic phenomenon was created. The consumer boom of the 50s and 60s, the extension of a **war economy** directly into the commercial sector, not only transformed the material living standards of the majority, it heralded at the same time, a comprehensive shift in the social structure of capitalism. The political and numerical predominance of a proletarian working class progressively diminished, to be replaced by a greater middle class.

Corporate Fordism was the natural beneficiary of a transformed, pre-war production-line economics. It had grown out from the manufacturing sector into new and burgeoning consumer markets. Its reliance on a Taylorist rationalisation of production, the imposition of new levels of labour efficiency through time and motion studies and upon forced economies of scale produced by the formation, by the purchase, of large brand conglomerates and trading franchises, required a progressive rationalisation of all functions of production throughout the economy. The war had been the catalyst to precipitate a revision of the mass production economy, opening new markets certainly but forcing new levels of pricing and higher levels of competitiveness on established industries.

Corporate Fordism came fully charged with its own managerial ethic, paradigmatically hierarchical and bureaucratic. It was above all a rigid and centralised organisation built around fiercely authoritarian relations. Architecture was an established service industry with its own ways of doing things. In the face of an unprecedented expansion of the building industry, in the sectors of sub-urban housing, commercial shopping and office space it was forced to accede to radical revisions of its forms of practice and social organisation. The acceptance of the new corporate Fordist terms was, of course, non-negotiable. Internal competition exacerbated the pace of change guaranteeing accession and compliance. Unlike the **heroic** Modernist revision of architectural practice which was predominantly formal, this time the restructuring of capital markets marked an irreversible shift in the way architecture was done socially. This time changes in aesthetic practices and formal procedures proved insufficient to ameliorate it.

Managerial corporatism became the **sine qua non** of managerial structures throughout all sectors of the economy including the increasingly important service economy of which architecture formed a significant part. Within the profession itself, corporatism was initially embraced by the largest firms and with spectacular results; the largest practices ever assembled emerged during this period, SOM being only the most notorious. Booming success however concealed the seeds of dissolution. Although the economy ripped away, from post-war expansion to cold war magnification, the erstwhile successes of the profession concealed a malignancy. Its assumed Fordist constituents – professionalism, pragmatism and a strict centralised bureaucracy – were absorbed, magically, into a trite formal pragmatism. Pragmatic functionalism, more of a managerial ideology than a demonstrable architectural style, although by now truly internationalist was also thoroughly prosaic, dehumanising and cold to the point of alienation.

A price had been paid. Architecture had made its own diabolical Faustian agreement. Managerial and abstract, a product of administrative craft and disingenuous commercial plotting it permitted itself no self-disfigurement or internal critique whatsoever. The transmogrification of the independent bourgeois architect into the manager architect, coerced by the rise of a Fordist managerial class and a corporate managerial ideology, was now effectively complete. The compelling alliance of a critical avant-garde with a broader and more culturally informed professional body, the very root of Modernism's popular success, was recklessly dissolved. A challenging, critical, and essentially oppositional avant-garde, which performed a campaigning and socially vigilant role, was forcefully excommunicated from the holy circle of pragmatic builders, money managers and administrators, **real** men of the **real** world. It had no alternative but to re-invent itself.

THE POPS (Neue Begrifflichkeit)
By the end of the 60s a popular social reconstruction

was universally incorporated as a reactionary fragment of the radical left, most especially in the arts. But what postured as non-conformism and insurgency failed to precipitate any consequent changes in the social territories of capitalism. The expulsion of the **avant-garde** wrought dire consequences for the conditions of its own production. Without any supra-contextual referent, without that is, a productive social teleology, the **avant-garde** was free to float in an ocean of frenetic form making and wild idealisms. Socially directed research into the wider cultural or anthropological implications of architectural practice, typical of the work of the TECTON group, for example, or later, of the Independent Group, the Smithson's and later still of Cedric Price, had maintained keen associations with material issues of the everyday. Unfettered by this necessity and ultimately spurred by the general narcissistic disposition of the post-beat generation, a brave new 'Pop' **avant-garde** took flight.

Paper architecture became a palpable aspect of the Pop generation at the end of the 60s. Born of pop art, of the **Beats**, of the **happening**, of 68 and of a shameless a-political recuperation of the ideas of the Situationist International, it proved far less radical than its own dissimulating view of itself suggested then or now. Plug-in, demountable, de-territorialised, de-historicised, transient, nomadic, it marked out the antithesis of a mono-thematic, mono-functional Modernism, but only in vague outline. Fundamentally influenced by the radical movements of the period, it hastily exchanged any commitment to the active left and to a clear social teleology for a recuperating stratagem in which the seminal tendencies of the period were serially commodified as formal products for the burgeoning gallery market.

More intuition than calculation, more radical chic than radical politics, Pop for all its self-propagandising bravura initiated a latent architectural heterogeneity, a plurality of architectural possibilities and nuances which proved sufficient in themselves to destabilise the corporate modernist hegemony. It started the rot but from the comfort of a cutesey, tongue-in-cheek, parody of corporate Modernism. Its inverted alliance with the most radical tendencies of the new left, most especially with the S.I., – the manner in which it appropriated these ideas notwithstanding – left it precariously disconnected from any stabilising theoretical ground. Anti-intellectual, a-political and lacking any serious theoretical foundation it managed, nevertheless, to establish a wide degree of popular support and thereby to unsettle if not to ultimately dislodge the **status quo**.

It would be entirely wrong however to perceive the Pop phenomenon, such as it was, as a mere consequence of revisionist **avant-garde** tendencies, merely the recuperating mechanism of bourgeois taste. The self-propagandising, self-marketing ethic developed by these early gallery architects was to become an enduring feature of the operation of all marginal architectural production during the Post-Modern period. Nevertheless it is Pop's erstwhile commitment to an equivocating pluralism which marks it out as crypto-radical and as a harbinger of the changes to come, marks it out as a putative Post-Modern tendency.

POST-MODERNISM

The publication of two seminal and highly influential books in the mid 60s and early 70s, the much celebrated critiques of Robert Venturi – 'Complexity and Contradiction in Architecture' and of Colin Rowe/ Fred Koetter – 'Collage City' aimed at demystifying and criticising the hegemony of a formulaic and corporate Modernism as it had established itself after the Second World War. Now seen as the first proposition, and in many ways, the seminal ground of what came to be known as **Post-Modern** and as **Post-Modernism**,

both sustained an attack on the reducing singularities, of corporate Modernism itself, disavowing its centralised market strategies, in favour of a plural and historicist model of architectural form. Complexity, ambiguity, collage and fragmentation, were its formal MODUS OPERANDI.

Forming the city from ideal fragments culled from an ethnocentrically Western interpretation of architectural history and by means of an exclusively formalist exposition, this first phase of Post-Modernism established a central pluralising ethic. No more single aspect, tunnel vision Modernism. These singular visions, the so-called meta-narratives of a Modernist ideology, disclaimed initially by the post-structuralist reformation in France, were progressively diminished and replaced by a comprehensive shift to heterogeneity, divergence and variance, terminating in a comprehensive muti-valency.

POST-FORDISM

To conclude that the well spring of Post-Modernist thought, or indeed Post-Modern architecture itself was a direct product of the speculations of these few architects and theorists would be a clear distortion. Demands for a broader cultural perspective, which might embrace peripheral, non-conformist and minority interests gathered pace from the mid-60s, evident initially in the areas of advertising and television. The critic Marshall McLuhan having exposed the political role of technological form, the coercive gloss of the technological media themselves, over what they merely communicated, unwittingly initiated a concerted hypostatisation of their influence as a market catalyst. Demands for a greater autonomy for marginal interests, which constituted a serious political critique of the centralising hegemony of Western capitalism in general and of corporate Fordism in particular, were ameliorated by a further and more socially withering economic revision.

During the 70s the economies of West Europe, the United States and the Pacific Rim experienced the beginnings of a dramatic shift in their capital structures. In contradistinction to the centralising tendencies of corporate Fordism, a more plauralising decentralised economic tendency, what has come to be known as 'post-Fordism', gathered pace. Characterised by a precipitous decline in heavy industrial and manufacturing production and by a compensating expansion of the service sector, this was most importantly a supra-national shift in the way that economies interacted and affected each other. What distinguished this phenomenon most strikingly was the role of the new communications technologies and their relative acceleration and extension of conditions of exchange. Dramatically improved communications fostered greater market sensitivity and, by degrees, a progressive fragmentation of market production, catering for ever finer differences in consumer taste.

The city was now post-modern. It had entred a new ideologically and culturally distinct era. It was post-industrial. It had established new conditions of capital production. It was post-Fordist. It had revised the nature of capital markets from centralised to plauralised. It was above all Post-Modern in so far as it embodied the liberal idealism of the new economics; inclusive, simultaneous, contextual, democratic, anti-Communist, but above all multi-valent and plural. No longer an indivisible and singular ideological construct the city and its animating markets was now a collection of differences. And just as plurality became the slogan for a rapid shift into market fragmentation it was established within architecture as a re-invigorating revision of an ossified and alienating Modernism.

The Venturi/Rowe initiative assimilated the post-Fordist revision into urban and architectural terms. An exclusively a-political and formalist assimilation, the new Post-Modern city was conceptually a city of complexity, collage and superimposition. Adopted as totems of an insinuated social engineering, the ideals of an anti-Communist, liberal democracy were assumed to inhere in examples of Europe's foremost architectural achievements. In a move of breathtaking naivete, conceptions of an aggregated rebus of appropriate precedents, effectively a collage city of remedial urban tissue, was offered as a panacea for healing the ailing Modernist city. Its justifying argument: that an environment which conforms to the highest formal values so called, will subtend the highest social values. A guileless conclusion which conveniently forgets that the Greek Polis required slave labour for its architecture and that it was used with open consent. An effective programmatic critique of the contemporary city, now in the throws of a post-Fordist economic revision, necessarily failed to materialise. A split in the protean Post-Modernist ranks ensued.

Funky enclave distribution; arbitrary image No. 1776.

But this was no political parting of the ways. The Po-Mos were not split on issues of political or social teleology, but on issues of form and the themes of production. Two tendencies emerged, firstly neo-Rationalism and then, belatedly in the late 70s, Deconstruction(ism). Whilst the later made a full-blooded return to an architecture of the object, neo-Rationalism hardened the initial Venturi/Rowe thrust. In the custom of anti-modern cultural pessimism, Rossi, the brothers Krier and the neo-Rationalist tendency in general, tightened the formal tourniquet of a proscribing historicism from its inaugural position of regressive utopianism to a revisionist and prosaic, neo-classicism.

The popular view of Deconstruction(ism), or Decon as it is more colloquially known, portrays it as an heroic return to the concerns of Modernism proper. And to a certain extent this was true, but only of its formal interests. Its representative cohort Tschumi, Eisenman, Koolhaas, even Libeskind, who studied with Dalibor Vesely, and Zaha Hadid, who studied with Leon Krier, were effectively converts to and not authors of the new creed. In point of fact Decon had no intellectual origin, in the sense in which Modernism morally opposed the excesses of nineteenth-century plagiarism. What characterises it most strongly as Post-Modern and as a surreptitious confederate of the Venturi/Rowe axis is... **firstly** a formal dependency on historical reference such as the Suprematist and neo-Plastic traditions, rather than upon any programmatic analysis of the immanent conditions of contemporary culture.

Secondly that it depended upon a formal and **imaginative** even arbitrary elaboration of extrinsic sources such as Chomsky, Derrida, Deleuze and Nietzsche, among others, as sufficient motive for subsequent production, obviating any thoroughgoing internal critique of its own means of production. And **thirdly**, that it was exclusively formalist in its

approach to the city, lacking any explicit political teleology or contemporary theory of the social body, beyond a vague assertion that novelty was itself intrinsically emancipating.

Contradicting a faith in the permanent values of the city as historical object there is a counter-faith in variance, invention and sheer difference. But this is merely the inverse of the same chronocentric obsession. Hypostasising the past as primogenitor, neo-Rationalism indulged a reification of history as tectonic social memory. Deconstruction is merely its obverse impression. Constructing a proleptical Futurism, of sorts, in which a presumed future is treated as already present, the quality of form and its novelty, were presumed to engender an emancipatory subversion. This disingenuous exchange of a chronological teleology for a social cause precluded any prospective closing of architectural ranks. Indeed, it proved to be entirely unnecessary. When a

liberative social **frisson** is assumed to be the product of a willful, even neurotic formalising, no focused theoretical trajectory or critical alignment is likely to emerge.

Decon had expanded the prospective Po-Mo product line adding crypto-Modernism to its neo-Classical merchandise. It was, however, much more heterogeneous than its neo-Rationalist counterpart and necessarily so. In a more sympathetic embrace of the hardening conditions of post-Fordism, Decon proliferated a series of neoteric architectural forms characterised by their specificity, exoticism and irreproducibility.

A designed environment of apparent chaos has to be predicated on precise technical control of the object....

The **frisson** of a formalised chaos does not subtend the social freedom it seems to embody. According to the late Robin Evans the whole procedure is anachronistic, he continues:

> The greater the control, the greater the phantasm of release produced by it, an old formula for cathartic art that still applies.
> — The Projective Cast

Sheer novelty characterised an economy in which style was reduced to autographic inscription. The prescient term **signature architecture**, rudely but effectively identified a lack of any shared principles amongst its disciples; of any united front, political or otherwise and of any discernible or consistent theoretical centre. But, then, Decon was always and already a result of the new economics, fiercely embodying a comprehensive fragmentation of architectural production.
Its adherents, after all, were initially paper architects, dependent upon the economy of a virtual notoriety to supply what a lack of practical experience could not. A reduction of the conventional distance between architecture and author abruptly followed. Without

Field drawing; territories of compulsory pleasure series; glass enclosure, Glienicke Park, Berlin, 1995.

a shared teleology or allying credo, and shouldering the influence of a universal social narcissism, the two became inseparable. Architect and architecture fused into a single aesthetic object, completing a general collapse into commodity strategies. If the Post-Modern had indeed materialised what Fredric Jameson refers to as "... **the consumption of sheer commodification as a process**...", then Deconstruction(ism), as far as architecture was concerned at any rate, was its terminal reification.

Partly as a consequence of its inclusive and uncritical formalism, partly out of hubris, but mostly out of **chagrin** for its own lack of an intrinsic theoretical centre, Decon played cultural hard ball with a gamut of extrinsic influences. After Heidegger, Derrida was its preeminent victim. But it was an elitist Nietzscheanism which was unconsciously insinuated. Whilst the construction of a working consensus amongst the Decon **avant-garde** remained anathema

given its free-market affiliations, competition in the sense of a formalist potlatch, a kind of bidding-up of the formal spectacle, prevailed as the ultimate basis of its cultural economy.

Deconstruction(ism), has bred the materially disengaged and politically weak architectures of the 80s and 90s. To a large extent, although it masquerades as a discrete phenomenon with its own identity, it is, **de facto**, merely a point along a continuous line of social transmogrification and cultural accommodation, subordinated ultimately to the material changes in the economic base. The narcissistic identification of architects with **their** architecture fabricates a confederation of two singularly powerful late-capitalist shibboleths – personality and commodity. This **signature architecture** remains well within the moral orbit of a neo-Nietzschean **will to power**; a fascoid liberal analgesic which fosters the passive view that within a culture of

trading individuals aesthetic manipulation is sufficient and from a moral standpoint preferable, to achieve professional success without political risk.

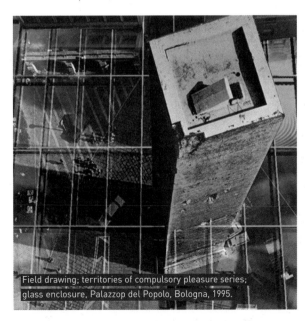

Field drawing; territories of compulsory pleasure series; glass enclosure, Palazzop del Popolo, Bologna, 1995.

Field drawing, territory series; No. 0113: plan.

Field drawing, territory series; No. 0156: plan.

Field drawing, territory series; No. 0318: plan.

Field drawing, territory series;
No. 0710: perspective.

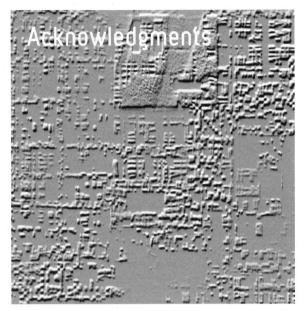
Acknowledgements

Participating students, Urbanism in the Extended Field. Winter semester 1995–1996 TU Berlin.
Thomas Poeschel, Diane Grunert, Petra Schriever, Ilies Rudolf, Jens Bauermeister, Gunnar Ring, Heike Krauss, Thomas Klink, Frits Optenberg, Carsten Kreuels, Vlatisa Seremet, Jan Braker, Heidrun Schuhmann, Boris Elzenheimer, Bettina Grothe, Irene Hüttenrauch, Agnieszka Kociemska, Gerold Esser, Moran McKay, Stephen Bohne, Kerstin Befan, Jan Blaurock, Birgit Schönbrodt, Jan Hübner, Esther Giani, Moxilka Deppe, Sandra Schneider, Frank Menzel, Karl Tomic, Heike Pell, Babett Holineck, Anja Nölken, Jurgen Rebstein, Heike Algner, Clare Gaffney

Participating students, 'Black Sea Coast Leisure Development'. Summer semester 1997 TU Berlin.
Richmute Lainge, Bettina Koenen, Anke Pipenstock, Tobias Wolf, Keon-Ho, Roland Sander, Jenny Sieg, Mathias Arnold, Jan Kowalewski, Martin Kruger, Soeren Eitel, Joseph Hamm, Christoph Stolzenberg

Special thanks to the following:
The members of Project X Belgrade. This group in a context impossible to imagine in west Europe are struggling to establish a strong architectural debate for a young and highly motivated group of Serbian architects in one of the world's most intriguing cities.

Acknowledgements
Many thanks to those who have participated in the production of this book. To my seminar and diploma students at the Technische Universität Berlin 1995–1997, for their diligent efforts in producing some of the work included and for struggling with difficult ideas in a general atmosphere that was often indifferent to them; to Project X Belgrade for their positivism in the face of serious and very real difficulties and for beginning the work on issues of field entrainment; to Deryk Dyne for his teachings on Freud and for his strenuous efforts to redirect my interests towards a productive end and to Duncan McCorquodale, the publisher of Serial Books, without who's initiative and persistence this volume would not have seen the light of day. Most especially thanks to my wife, Janette Emery, for her endless patience which fostered a thorough and productive critique of all aspects of this book and for her invaluable help in pre-editing large sections of the text. Work included was broached, prepared discussed and variously revised over a five year period at a number of universities including the Bartlett School of Architecture, University College London, University of Westminster London, the Technische Universität Berlin, the Hochschule für Gestaltung, Berlin, Weisensee; the Staedl Schule, Frankfurt; the Technical University, Belgrade; the Museum of Folk Arts and Handicrafts, Belgrade; the Technical University, Sofia.

Participants in the workshop 'Flow city, Belgrade' Museum of Arts and Crafts, Belgrade 1997; in association with Project X Belgrade.
Projekt X: Milica Topalovic, Ana Dzokic, Maja Bulatovic, Sasa Budimir, Gordana Dunic, Emina Petrovic, Ljubica Bulatovic.
Associated participants: Marija Krtinic, Marko Jobst, Viktor Jovanovic, Natalija Miodragovic, Katarina Mrkonjic, Ana Nikezic, Uros Vukovic, Nebojsa Adzic, Ivana Filipovic, Marija Milinkovic, Igor Marjanovic.

Participants in the workshop 'Visions for Sarajevo' Seidle Villa, Munich, 1996; in association with the Technical University Munich.
Sebastian Wagner, Christine Diekmann, Daniel Fehrmann, Christopher Fricke, Beatrice Gilini, Boris Radczun, Christoph Schuseil, Lukjas Weder, Annett Zinsmeister.

Participating students, Leipzig project. Summer semester 1996 TU Berlin.
Christine Dissmann, Beatrice Giulini, Daniel Tehrmann, Karl Tamilx, Boris Radlzun, Lukas Weder, Dietmar Otto, Alexander Sarges, Torsten Schulze, Nicole Martin, Lilian Jüchtern

Participating students, 'Vienna/Bratislava Connector'. Winter semester 1996–1997 TU Berlin.
Andreas Hoelemann, Herbert Klitzsch, Ralph Heckersbruch, Florian Boxberg, Patrick Niesert, Philipp Reinfeld, Michael Heim

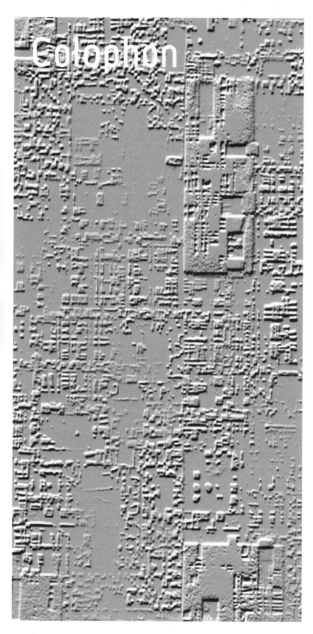

Colophon

All opinions expressed in material contained within this publication are those of the authors and not necessarily those of the editor or publisher.

© 1999 Black Dog Publishing Limited and the authors.
Edited and produced by Duncan McCorquodale.
Designed by Christian Küsters.

Printed in the European Union.

ISBN 1 901033 40 6

British Library cataloguing-in-publication data. A catalogue record for this book is available from the British Library.
Library of Congress cataloguing-in-publication data:
Field Event/Field Space.
Kevin Rhowbotham.

The Serial Books Architecture & Urbanism series is kindly supported by the Alvin Boyarsky Memorial Trust.

Titles available in the series include
Boyarsky + Murphy's Action Research and
Tom Verebes + Michael Hensel's .urbanisations .O.C.E.A.N. UK .

For further information concerning other titles in the Serial Books Architecture & Urbanism series please contact Black Dog Publishing Limited in writing.

Black Dog Publishing Limited
PO Box 3082
London NW1 UK